STAFFORD
TO CHESTER

Vic Mitchell and Keith Smith

MP Middleton Press

Front cover: No. 85016 is arriving at platform 5 at Crewe on 3rd October 1987, with the 14.25 Liverpool to Birmingham. The class 85s were built at Doncaster in 1961-64. A full brake van always separated the Mk I coaches. (H.Ballantyne)

Back cover upper: A rare sight was the Advanced Passenger Train. No. 370005 runs south through platform 3 at Crewe at 09.20 on 2nd April 1985. Soon to be withdrawn, many of the APT coaches can now be seen at the nearby Heritage Centre. (P.Jones)

Back cover lower: Recreating the late 1930s, no. 6233 Duchess of Sutherland *leaves Crewe on 13th April 2002, with a special train from Derby to Blackpool. Much historic steelwork is in the background. (H.Ballantyne)*

Published November 2012

ISBN 978 1 908174 34 5

© Middleton Press, 2012

Design Deborah Esher
Typesetting Barbara Mitchell

Published by
  Middleton Press
  Easebourne Lane
  Midhurst
  West Sussex
  GU29 9AZ
Tel: 01730 813169
Fax: 01730 812601
Email: info@middletonpress.co.uk
www.middletonpress.co.uk

Printed in the United Kingdom by Henry Ling Limited, at the Dorset Press, Dorchester, DT1 1HD

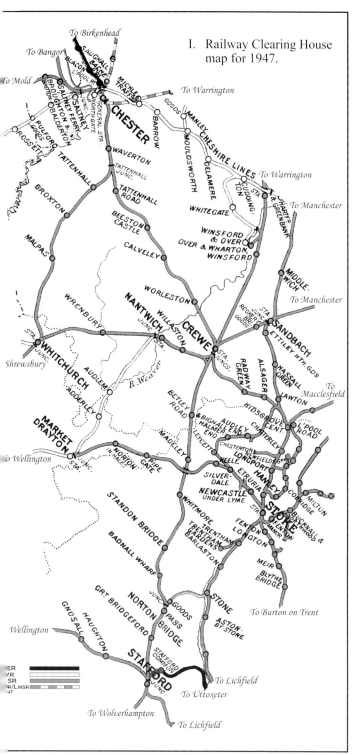

I. Railway Clearing House map for 1947.

ACKNOWLEDGEMENTS

We are very grateful for the assistance received from many of those mentioned in the credits also to A.R.Carder, A.J.Castledine, G.Croughton, S.C.Jenkins, N.Langridge, B.Lewis, J.P.McCrickard, B.I.Nathan, Mr D. and Dr S.Salter, M.J.Stretton, T.Walsh and in particular, our always supportive wives, Barbara Mitchell and Janet Smith.

GEOGRAPHICAL SETTING

The county town and important commercial centre of Stafford is situated on a waterway known as the River Sow. Our route follows this up stream to Norton Bridge and thence follows the Meece Brook, a tributary of the River Sow. The summit of the line is reached after a further ten miles, near Madeley, after which it passes from Staffordshire into Cheshire East.

Six lines still radiate from the railway town of Crewe, which had about 200 residents until the trains arrived. It has no geographical features of note. About three miles west of it, we pass over the River Weaver and then the Shropshire Union Canal.

The remainder of the journey is close to this and across the fairly level Cheshire Plain. We end our trip at another important county town, Chester. It is situated on bends on the River Dee, which flows from the south and enters the sea several miles west of the city.

Most of the route was built over red sandstones, although the area near the summit passes through mudstone.

The maps are to the scale of 25ins to 1 mile, with north at the top, unless otherwise indicated.

Gradient Profile

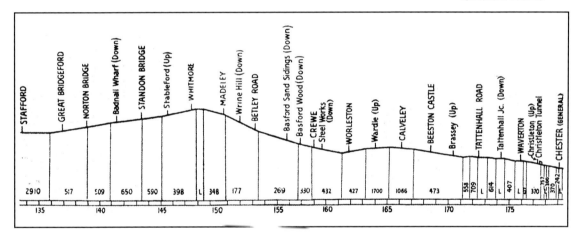

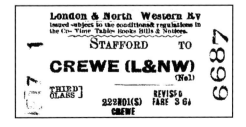

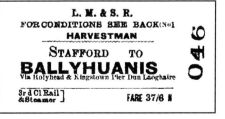

HISTORICAL BACKGROUND

The Grand Junction Railway opened from Birmingham, through Stafford and Crewe to Warrington on 4th July 1837. The line from Crewe to Chester came into use on 1st October 1840. These routes formed a large part of the London & North Western Railway, upon its creation in 1846.

The connecting passenger lines, from south to north, opened as follows: From Lichfield to Stafford in 1847, from Wellington to Stafford in 1849 (closed 1966), from Uttoxeter to Stafford in 1867 (closed 1939) and from Stoke-on-Trent in 1848. Crewe had connections with Manchester from 1842, Nantwich from 1858 and also Kidsgrove from 1858. There were trains to Tattenhall Junction from Whitchurch between 1872 and 1964. Chester had services to Birkenhead from 1840, to Wrexham from 1846, to Bangor from 1848, to Mold from 1849 (until 1962) and to Warrington from 1850. Other trains used Chester Northgate terminus between 1875 and 1969.

The LNWR became part of the London Midland & Scottish Railway in 1923. This largely became the London Midland Region of British Railways upon nationalisation in 1948.

Following the Railways Act of November 1993, privatisation resulted in five operating companies usually providing the service between Stafford and Crewe, with two working to Chester. Most began in 1997, but the franchise durations have varied.

Electrification

This began on the West Coast Main Line from Crewe to Manchester on 12th September 1960 and between Crewe and Liverpool on 1st January 1962. The new standard of 25kV at 50 cycles was used. Stafford to Crewe electric services began on 7th January 1963 and they reached London on 6th November 1965. Birmingham was served from 5th December 1966 and Preston from 23rd July 1973.

Widening

Stafford - Norton Bridge (Up line)	1874
Stafford - Norton Bridge (Down line)	1876
Norton Bridge - Whitmore (Both lines)	1876
Whitmore - Crewe (Both lines)	1875

There was quadruple track through Crewe station from 1848.

PASSENGER SERVICES

The tables below indicate the number of down trains (northwards) in sample years. Initially, the calling patterns were irregular. The figures in brackets show the number of trains listed which called at most of the intermediate stations. Those running on less than five days per week are not shown; neither are those not stopping at Crewe or Stafford.

	Stafford to Crewe Weekdays	Stafford to Crewe Sundays	Crewe to Chester Weekdays	Crewe to Chester Sundays
1841	7	4	4	4
1850	6	4	6	2
1865	14(3)	6(1)	11(4)	5(1)
1895	16(4)	8(0)	14(5)	5(1)
1922	17(3)	5(0)	21(5)	5(1)
1951	23(2)	15(0)	18(5)	9(0)
1980	19	11	20	14
2012	39	22	30	30

The final figures include the many sleeper services over the routes.

July 1847

London & North Western.—LIVERPOOL & BIRMINGHAM Section. Treasurer, Thos. Goalen.

Dist.	LONDON TO LIVERPOOL & CARLISLE.	8¾ p.m. Mail Mixed	6 a.m. 1 & 2 class	6¼ a.m. Mixed Mail	8½ a.m. 1st cl. mixed	10 a.m. Exprs Mail.	7 a.m. 3rd cl. only.	11 a.m. 1st cl. mixed	12½ p.m. 1 & 2 class	5 p.m. Express
Mls.	**London,** Euston Sq.	8 45	..	6 15	8 30	10 0	7 0	11 0	12 30	5 0
112½	**Birmingham....**	1 25	6	11¼	1	1¾	3½	4¼	6	8 10
115¾	Perry Bar	..	6 9	..	..	..	3 41	..	6 8	..
119¼	Newton Road	..	6 18	..	..	..	3 53	..	6 17	..
122	**Walsall**	1 50	6 28	11 37	1 22	..	4 4	4 38	6 26	..
124½	Willenhall..........	..	6 36	..	1 32	..	4 14	..	6 34	..
127	**Wolverhampton**	2 0	6 45	11 52	1 40	2 13	4 24	4 50	6 42	8 34
132½	Four Ashes	..	6 59	..	..	..	4 43	..	6 55	..
134	Spread Eagle	..	7 6	..	..	..	4 51	..	7 2	..
138½	Penkridge..........	..	7 14	12 7	..	..	5 0	5 10	7 10	..
141¾	**Stafford**..........	2 28	7 25	12 20	2 10	2 41	5 17	5 24	7 22	9 3
147½	Norton Bridge......	..	7 41	..	2 25	..	5 55	..	7 38	..
155¾	**Whitmore** * ..	3 0	8 2	12 55	2 49	3 14	6 32	6 0	8 1	..
159	Madeley............	..	8 10	..	..	..	6 45	..	8 10	..
163½	Basford............	..	8 22	..	..	..	7 31	6 17	8 22	..
166¼	**Crewe**	3 25	8 28	1 19	3 12	3 35	7 39	6 24	8 28	9 47
171¾	Minshull Vernon ..	..	8 42	..	..	..	8 1	..	8 42	..
173¾	Winsford		8 50	..	3 29	..	8 10	..	8 50	..
178¼	**Hartford**	3 59	9 1	1 44	3 41	3 50	8 24	6 51	9 1	..
180¾	Acton..............	..	9 9	..	..	..	8 35	..	9 9	..
185	Preston Brook......	..	9 22	2 0	..	..	8 49	..	9 22	..
187½	Moore	.	9 31	..	..	..	8 58	..	9 31	..
190½	**Warrington**	4 27	9 38	2 16	4 5	4 19	9 16	7 18	9 38	10 25
195¼	Newton Bridge	4 47	10 0	2 38	..	4 43	..	..	..	..
210	**Liverpool**........	5 25	10 45	3 15	5 0	5 10	10 30	8 15	10 45	11 10
197	**Chester**..........	4 21	9 46	2 26	..	4 38	9 10	8 5	9 40	10 35
218¼	**Preston**..........	5 39	12 10	3 35	..	5 30	..	..	..	11 30
307¾	**Carlisle**..........	10 4	..	7 50	..	9 55	..	.	..	..

Dist.	LONDON TO LIVERPOOL & CARLISLE.	Sunday Trains. p.m. mix. mail	Sunday Trains. a.m. mix. & 3cl	Sunday Trains. a.m. mix. Mail.	Sunday Trains. a.m. Exp Mail.	Fares frm Birming. By 1¾ p.m. & Expres	Fares frm Birming. 1st Class	Fares frm Birming. 2nd Cls.	Fares frm Birming. 3rd Cls.
Mls.	**London,** Euston Sq.	8 45	..	..	10 0				
112½	**Birmingham....**	1 25	7½	11¼	1¾	s. d.	s. d.	s. d.	s. d.
115¾	Perry Bar	..	..	..	..	....	0 8	0 6	0 4
119¼	Newton Road	..	..	..	..	....	1 2	0 9	0 7
122	**Walsall**	1 50	7 49	11 37	..	....	1 8	1 0	0 10
124½	Willenhall..........	..	..	..	..	....	2 0	1 6	1 0
127	**Wolverhampton**	2 0	8 5	11 52	2 13	2 9	2 6	1 9	1 3
132½	Four Ashes	..	..	..	..	....	3 6	2 [illegible]	1 8
134	Spread Eagle	..	..	..	..	....	4 0	2 9	1 10
138½	Penkridge..........	..	..	..	..	....	4 6	3 0	2 0
141¾	**Stafford**..........	2 28	8 30	12 17	2 41	5 6	5 0	4 0	2 6
147½	Norton Bridge......	..	..	..	..	....	6 0	4 6	2 11
155¾	**Whitmore** * ..	3 0	9 8	12 55	3 14	9 0	7 6	5 6	3 8
159	Madeley............	..	..	..	..	....	8 0	6 0	3 10
163½	Basford............	..	..	..	..	....	9 6	6 6	4 4
166¼	**Crewe**	3 25	9 32	1 19	3 35	11 0	9 6	7 0	4 6
171¾	Minshull Vernon ..	..	..	..	..	....	10 0	7 6	4 11
173¾	Winsford	..	..	..	..	....	10 6	8 0	5 2
178¼	**Hartford**	3 59	9 57	1 44	3 56	14 0	11 0	8 6	5 6
180¾	Acton..............	..	..	..	..	....	11 6	8 6	5 9
185	Preston Brook......	..	..	..	..	....	12 6	9 0	6 1
187½	Moore	..	..	..	..	....	13 0	9 6	6 3
190½	**Warrington**	4 27	10 25	2 16	4 19	17 0	13 6	10 0	6 6
195¼	Newton Bridge	4 47	..	..	4 43	..	14 0	10 6	6 11
210	**Liverpool**........	5 25	11 30	3 15	5 10	20 0	17 0	13 0	8 2
197	**Chester**..........	4 21	..	..	4 38	15 6	13 0	9 6	6 3
218¼	**Preston**..........	5 39	..	..	5 30	..	..	..	....
307¾	**Carlisle**..........	10 4	..	..	9 55	..	..	..	....

CHESTER AND CREWE BRANCH—21 Miles in length.

From Chester	STATIONS.	Mail Exp. a.m.	1 & 2 class. a.m.	3rd Class only. a.m.	1st Class. mixed a.m.	1 & 2 mixed a.m.	1st Class. Mixed, a.m.	Ex-prs. trn. p.m	1 & 2 cls. p.m	Mail. Mixed. p.m.
Mls	Birkenhead	..	6 15	..	8 45	9 45	10 45	3 45	3 45	8 45
—	CHESTER........	6 28	7 0	8 30	9 45	10 30	11 40	5 10	5 20	9 22
3	Waverton........	..	..	8 45	..	10 46	..	..	5 32	..
7	Tattenhall	..	7 15	9 4	10 2	10 48	11 55	..	5 43	..
10½	Beeston..........	6 52	7 20	9 24	10 14	11 1	12 5	..	5 55	9 46
13	Calveley	..	7 31	9 36	10 21	11 10	12 12	..	6 5	..
17	Nantwich	..	7 45	9 56	10 33	11 23	12 22	..	6 14	..
21	CREWE	7 20	8 0	10 15	10 48	11 36	12 38	5 50	6 26	10 2
75	Manchester......	..	10 0	..	..	1 10	2 35	..	8 0	..
	Birmingham	9 15	11 0	1 50	1 15	..	3 20	7 35	10 0	12 36

From Birmng	STATIONS.	Mail. mixd. a.m.	1 & 2 class. a.m.	a.m.	Mail. mixd. a.m.	Mail. p.m.	3rd class, only. p.m.	1st cls. Mix p.m	1 & 2 cls. p.m	Ex prss p.m
Mls	Birmingham ..	1 25	6 0	..	11 15	1 45	3 30	4 15	6 0	8 10
	Manchester ..	..	7 0	10 0	11 30	..	..	5 15	..	..
54	CREWE	3 25	8 40	11 30	1 19	3 41	7 50	7 0	8 35	9 47
58	Nantwich	..	8 51	11 41	1 31	..	8 6	7 11	8 46	..
62	Calveley	..	9 4	11 54	1 44	..	8 20	7 24	9 0	..
64½	Beeston........	3 55	9 13	12 3	1 53	4 4	8 30	7 33	9 7	..
68	Tattenhall	..	9 26	12 16	2 6	..	8 45	7 46	9 20	..
72	Waverton......	..	9 36	..	2 18	..	8 55	7 54	..	..
75	CHESTER......	4 21	9 46	12 36	2 26	4 38	9 10	8 5	9 40	10 35
91	Birkenhead	4 40	11 15	2 15	4 0	5 40	..	9 15	..	11 10

Mail trains only run on Sundays. FARES. Chester to Crewe 4s. by express.—3s. 6d.—3s.—1s. 9d.—Manchester to Chester, 8s. 6d.—6s.—4s. 4d.

* For Coaches in connexion with this station, see page 71.

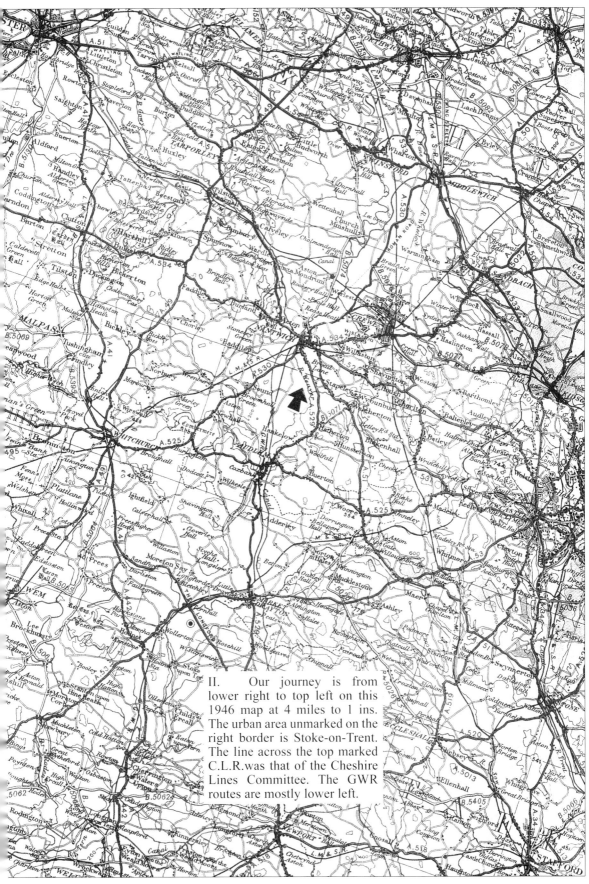

II.   Our journey is from lower right to top left on this 1946 map at 4 miles to 1 ins. The urban area unmarked on the right border is Stoke-on-Trent. The line across the top marked C.L.R. was that of the Cheshire Lines Committee. The GWR routes are mostly lower left.

STAFFORD

III.   The 1921 map at 6 ins to 1 mile has the Wellington line curving west, our route to Crewe running northwest from the station and the Great Northern Railway's line to Uttoxeter at the top right corner of the extract. The two engine sheds are northwest of the station; the earlier two were southeast of it, beyond the edge of the map and near Trent Valley Junction.

1.   The first station lasted until 1844 and here we see the third, which was created in 1861-62. On the right is the Station Hotel. (P.Laming coll.)

2.   Rebuilding in the early 1860s brought fine long roofs over the main platforms and they appear from different angles in the following four photographs. This one includes 2-2-2-0 no. 610 in about 1904. (R.S.Carpenter coll.)

3. The complexity of the glazed roofing is apparent as we find a North Staffordshire Railway train in the bay platform on the right. Its destination will be Uttoxeter. (J.K.Williams coll.)

4. This postcard record is near the main entrance towards the end of the 19th century. The telegraph office was much used prior to telephones. The railway's lineside wires were used to convey coded messages, which were written at each end of the transmission. (P.Laming coll.)

→ 5. We are at the north end of the station in about the 1930s, as LNER 0-6-0 no. 3623 leaves with a train bound for Uttoxeter and Derby. There is an LMS 0-6-0 on the right. (J.K.Williams coll.)

→ 6. Looking north on 19th September 1959, we can enjoy the ambience of the spacious platforms, uncluttered by columns. A van for parcels stands in the gloom behind the sign. (H.C.Casserley)

↘ 7. The station rebuilding started in 1960 and the official opening of the new premises took place on 31st December 1962. This is a view north after the wires had come into use in 1963. (Lens of Sutton coll.)

8. Speeding south to Euston is no. 86008 on 29th July 1978. There was a good view of the stopping trains from the well glazed footbridge.
(T.Heavyside)

9. The roar of an occasional diesel was still to be heard in 1998. Seen on 18th July is EW&S no. 37415 with the 17.21 Birmingham New Street to Holyhead, at platform 4. Platforms 1, 6 and 7 were signalled for reversible running, the latter (right) being devoted to Royal Mail traffic.
(R.F.Roberts/
SLS coll.)

10. Bearing the legend Virgin, no. 86212 was heading the 10.31 Birmingham International to Edinburgh on 22nd February 2001. The nameplate states *Preston Guild 1328-1992*.
(D.H.Mitchell)

11. The 15.04 Liverpool to Birmingham New Street was worked by no. 350104 on 11th July 2012 and is seen entering platform 4. These "Desiro" units were built by Siemens and were introduced on 13th June 2005. (H.Ballantyne)

Other views of this station can be found in pictures 103 to 120 in our *Rugby to Stafford* album, along with the signalling evolution story.

12. All traces of the original structure were lost during the reconstruction and here is the prospective passenger's perspective on 12th September 2012. The approach is much more spacious than that at Crewe. (H.Ballantyne)

13.　　Two engine sheds are shown on the map north of the down island platform from which this photograph was taken on 23rd August 1948. The coaling plant is behind the locomotive. (H.C.Casserley)

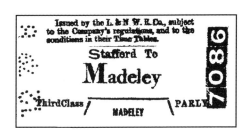

14.   Seen in the same month is ex-LNWR "Prince of Wales" class 4-6-0 no. 25648 *Queen of the Belgians*; its demise was imminent. The four-road shed was completed in 1852 and termed No. 1. No. 2 had six roads and came into use in 1861. (M.Whitehouse coll.)

15.   A record from 22nd April 1962 has no. 42976 facing us outside No. 2 shed, which had its triple hipped roof replaced by this one in 1947. The depot's final code was 5C and it closed on 19th July 1965. The sheds were later used for industrial purposes. (R.S.Carpenter)

16. Castle Street bridge is seen from the north, with the ex-GNR line to Uttoxeter on the left and the route to Newport on the right. Known as the Shropshire Union Line a one mile stub was retained after closure to take supplies to the Universal Abrasives' discharge pit. (J.K.Williams coll.)

17. A view of the same location, but in the opposite direction, has 4-6-0 no. 46145 *The Duke of Wellington's Regt. (West Riding)* about to pass under Castle Street on 14th April 1962. On the left is the fitting shop of W.G.Bagnall Ltd., where many narrow gauge locomotives were completed. (J.K.Williams coll.)

18. No. 5 Box was still in use on 20th July 2012, while a class 221 Voyager unit runs south under Castle Street bridge. The earlier box had been on the other side of the tracks. (H.Ballantyne)

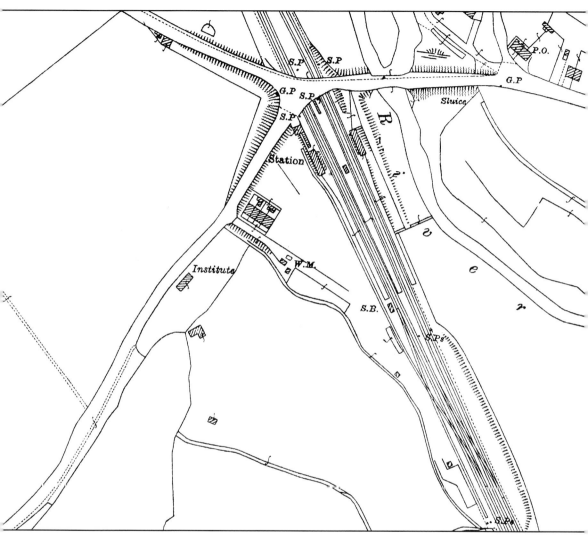

IV.   The 1923 edition shows only four staff cottages near to the station. The first platforms had been further north and were in use until 1840, being named simply BRIDGEFORD.

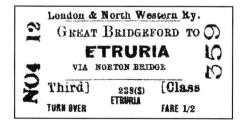

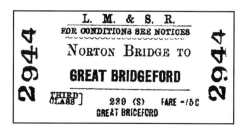

19.   A northward view in about 1940 shows white lines on the edges of the outer platforms, as they were the most used. The steps down from the road level booking office are obscured by the waiting room. Those to the island platform are evident; the right platform has a sloping path. (Stations UK)

20.   A southward panorama from the same era includes the goods yard, which closed on 22nd June 1959, and the signal box, which was not used after 8th October 1961. Passenger service ceased here on 8th August 1949, although trains continued to call for railway workers until 1952. (Stations UK)

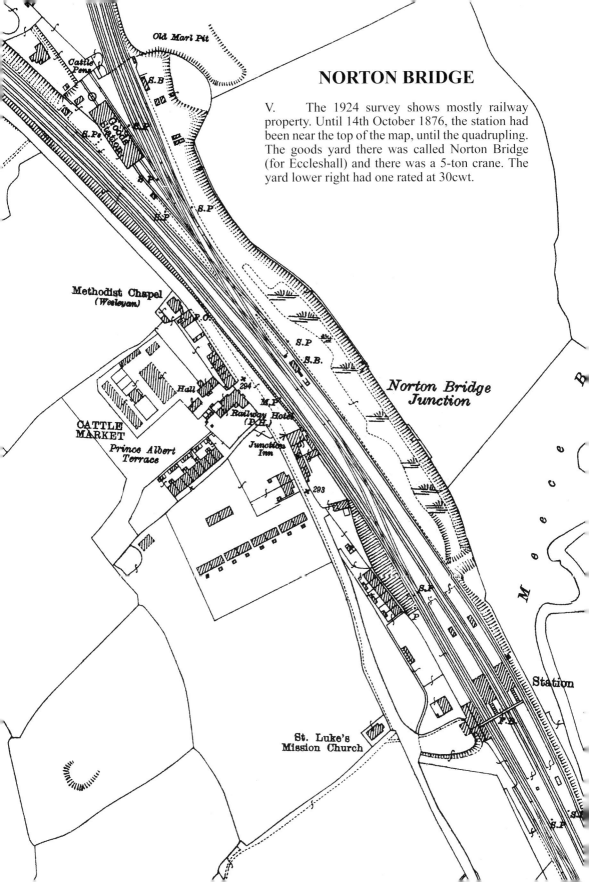

NORTON BRIDGE

V.   The 1924 survey shows mostly railway property. Until 14th October 1876, the station had been near the top of the map, until the quadrupling. The goods yard there was called Norton Bridge (for Eccleshall) and there was a 5-ton crane. The yard lower right had one rated at 30cwt.

Old Marl Pit

Cattle Pens

S.B.

Goods Station

S.P.

S.P.

S.P.

S.P.

Methodist Chapel
(Wesleyan)

Hall

S.P.

S.B.

Norton Bridge
Junction

294

M.P.

Railway Hotel
(P.H.)

CATTLE
MARKET

Prince Albert
Terrace

Junction
Inn

293

S.P.

P

St. Luke's
Mission Church

M
e
e
c
e

B

Station

P.B.

S.P.

S.P.

21. Major rebuilding took place at the time of the track quadrupling and this small structure was erected slightly above natural ground level. This allowed the footbridge to the platforms to be at the same level. (P.Laming coll.)

22. The building seen in the previous picture is upper left in this one. The dwelling on the right was probably the home of the station master. North of the station was a signal box, which was called Badnall Wharf. From 1880, there had been a siding with a goods wharf (see map II) to serve the village of Eccleshall. It closed on the 22nd June 1959. The box was replaced by a flat-roof ARP type with 100 levers. It opened on 3rd March 1940 and closed on 25th June 1967. The box controlled a new reception line and two lines serving an island platform (opened on 3rd August 1941), all for the new Royal Ordnance Factory at Swynnerton. (This was also served by a branch off the Norton Bridge - Stone line to Cold Meece station, built especially for the factory workers trains). The Badnall Wharf connections into the ROF were abolished on 1st August 1965. The sidings had been used for condemned locomotives in the 1950s. (Lens of Sutton coll.)

23.   A view south on 15th June 1957 features "Patriot" class 4-6-0 no. 45545 *Planet*, bound for the Stoke line. On the right of this and the next picture is the cattle dock. (Bentley coll.)

24.   Seen on the same day are nos 45634 *Trinidad* (left) and 2-6-4T no. 42449. The former was of the "Jubilee" class, introduced in 1934. (Bentley coll.)

25.   Another view from the footbridge that day is northwards and shows the up "Royal Scot", hauled by no. 10203, a rare diesel BR prototype, built at Brighton in 1954. (Bentley coll.)

26.   Further north, on the same day, we can enjoy the sight of "Royal Scot" class 4-6-0 no. 46161 *King's Own* speeding towards Crewe. In the background is the ex-LNWR signal box, which was in use until 11th December 1960. On the left is the spacious goods shed; its traffic ceased on 22nd June 1959. (Bentley coll.)

27.   There was a temporary signal box before this one opened on 8th October 1961; it closed on 28th June 2004. It is seen on 16th February 1995, with a stopping train at the short lived island platform. Trains have not called since 23rd May 2004, when the footbridge was deemed to have structural failure. Times continued to appear in timetables in 2012, but a bus called nearby. There had been eleven trains on weekdays each way until 2004. The class 37 is on the up slow line. (M.Turvey)

This is the signalling diagram, new in 1961. On the right, the Stafford lines from top to bottom are: up fast, down fast, up slow and down slow. The track below the new island platform was termed the "recess line". It was signalled for reversible running and could be used to hold any stopping train, thus avoiding delays to fast services. (Railway Magazine)

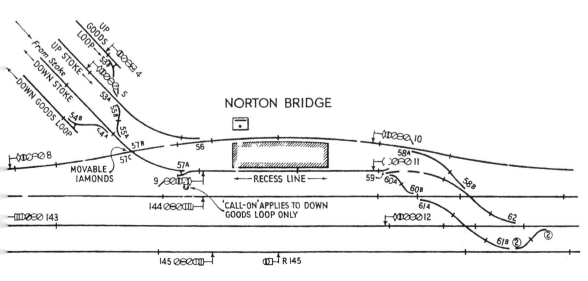

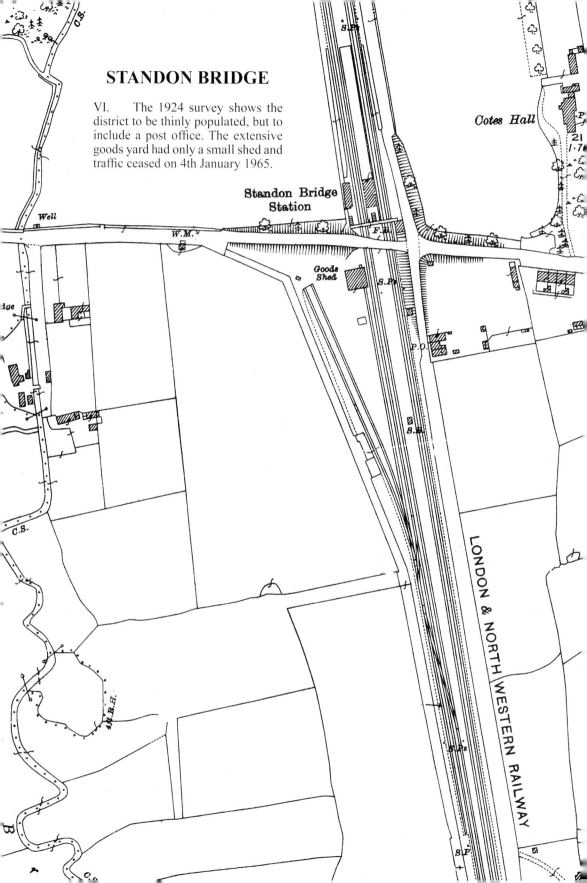

STANDON BRIDGE

VI.   The 1924 survey shows the district to be thinly populated, but to include a post office. The extensive goods yard had only a small shed and traffic ceased on 4th January 1965.

Cotes Hall

Standon Bridge
Station

Well

W.M.

Goods
Shed

S.P.

P.O.

S.B.

C.S.

LONDON & NORTH WESTERN RAILWAY

S.P.

28. A southward panorama includes another road level booking office, with steps down to the platform. In the distance is the signal box, which was in use until 8th October 1961. Further north was Stableford Box, which closed on the same day. (P.Laming coll.)

29. A 1949 view north includes the barrow crossing, which has just been used by the perambulator. Passenger traffic ceased on 4th February 1952. (Stations UK)

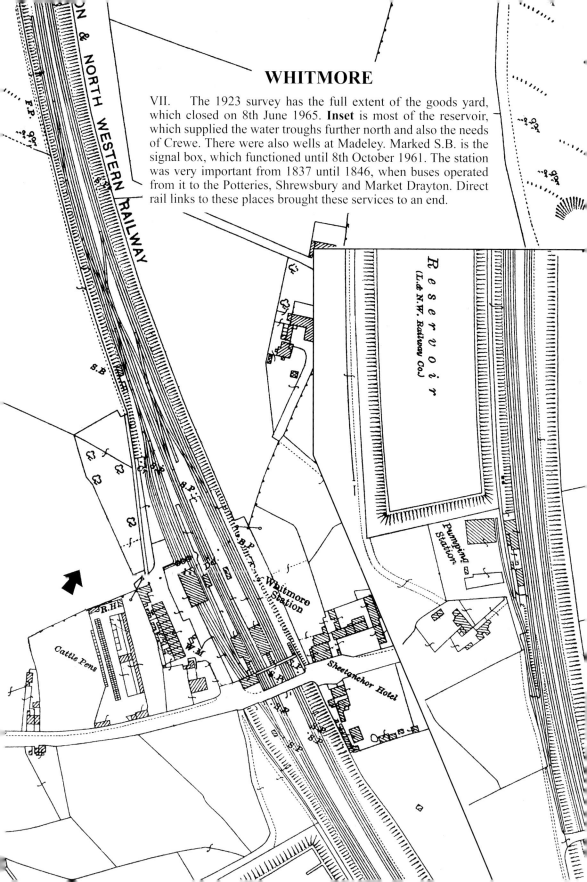

WHITMORE

VII.   The 1923 survey has the full extent of the goods yard, which closed on 8th June 1965. **Inset** is most of the reservoir, which supplied the water troughs further north and also the needs of Crewe. There were also wells at Madeley. Marked S.B. is the signal box, which functioned until 8th October 1961. The station was very important from 1837 until 1846, when buses operated from it to the Potteries, Shrewsbury and Market Drayton. Direct rail links to these places brought these services to an end.

30.   The "Coronation Scot" became a famous train for the LMS in the late 1930s, with the white bands running the full length of the train. No. 6223 *Princess Alice* is seen in 1938, running north. (Bentley coll.)

31.   An indifferent southward view from about 1947 has to suffice for the operational station, which closed on 4th February 1952. The population was only 645 in 1961, the village being one mile east along the A53. (Stations UK)

32.   It is 29th April 1966 and the new fleet of electric locomotives were hauling the BR Mk. I coaches from the steam era. The latter's maroon livery was similar to that of the LMS. The locomotive is a class 86, of which 100 were delivered in 1965-66.(Bentley coll.)

33.   A view south on 31st May 2003 includes the site of the goods yard on the right. Two sidings had once ended near the black wall below the former booking office. Passing is a class 87. (M.Turvey)

34. The summit level is almost one mile in length and this is where the LNWR established water troughs in the 1860s. Locomotives nos 1113 and 1304 were recorded running north. They were "Precursor" 4-4-0 and "Experiment" 4-6-0 respectively. (R.M.Casserley coll.)

35. Heading a down express on 7th June 1930 is no. 5335 *Miles MacInnes*, a "George the Fifth" class 4-4-0. Experienced passengers knew when to close the windows, if their train was at a good speed. (Bentley coll.)

36. Freight trains seldom needed water on the move. This example is hauled by 0-8-0 no. 9110, a 4F class G introduced in 1910. (R.M.Casserley coll.)

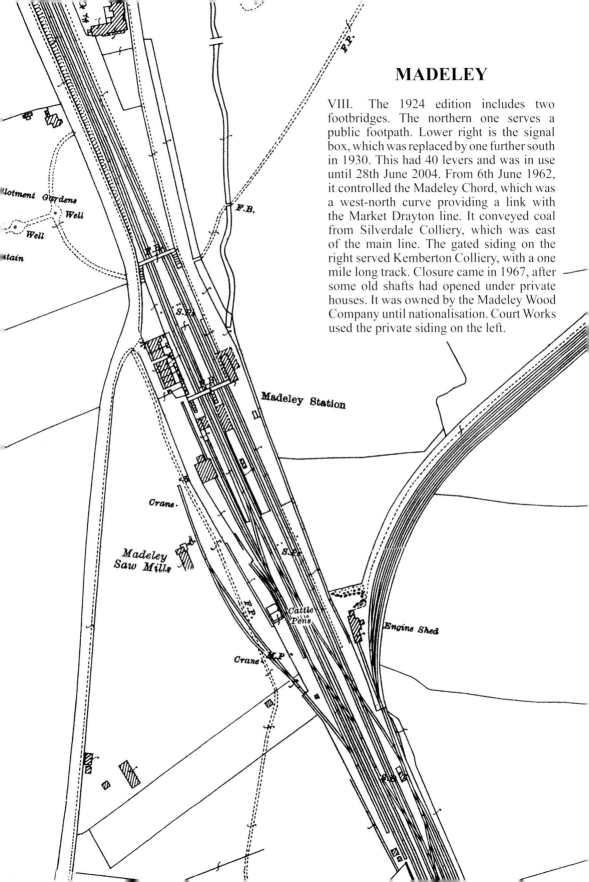

MADELEY

VIII. The 1924 edition includes two footbridges. The northern one serves a public footpath. Lower right is the signal box, which was replaced by one further south in 1930. This had 40 levers and was in use until 28th June 2004. From 6th June 1962, it controlled the Madeley Chord, which was a west-north curve providing a link with the Market Drayton line. It conveyed coal from Silverdale Colliery, which was east of the main line. The gated siding on the right served Kemberton Colliery, with a one mile long track. Closure came in 1967, after some old shafts had opened under private houses. It was owned by the Madeley Wood Company until nationalisation. Court Works used the private siding on the left.

F.P.

F.B.

llotment Gardens

Well

Well

tain

F.B.

S.B.

Madeley Station

Crane.

Madeley Saw Mills

S.B.

F.P.

Cattle Pens

Engine Shed

Crane

M.P.

F.B.

37.   A southward view from a poor postcard features the main building, the small engine shed and the tall signal box. Madeley was on the east side of the line and had a population of 2909 in 1901, this rising to 3444 by 1961. (P.Laming coll.)

38.   Moving back and onto the public footbridge, we find the goods shed in the panorama, on the right. Passenger traffic ceased here on 4th February 1952 and freight on 19th August 1963. (Lens of Sutton coll.)

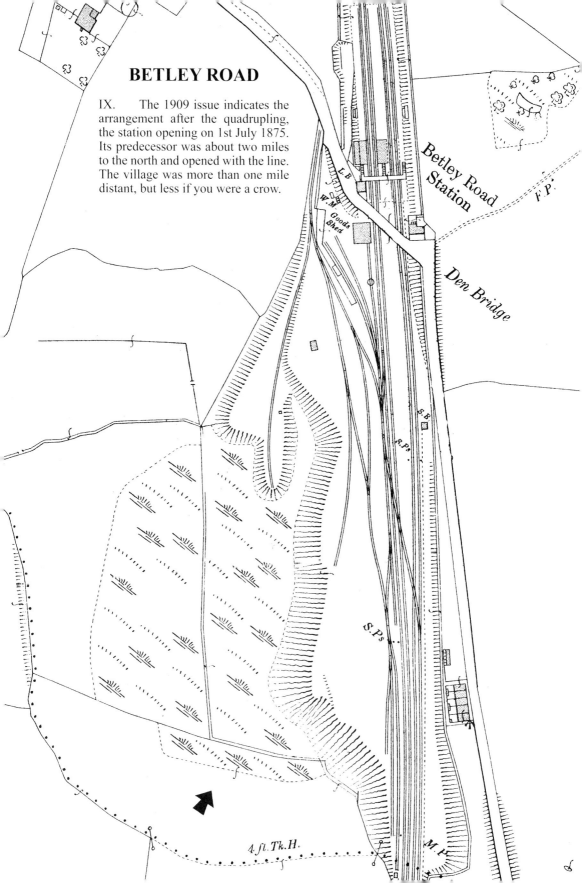

BETLEY ROAD

IX.   The 1909 issue indicates the arrangement after the quadrupling, the station opening on 1st July 1875. Its predecessor was about two miles to the north and opened with the line. The village was more than one mile distant, but less if you were a crow.

Betley Road Station

F.P.

Den Bridge

L B

W.M.

Goods Shed

S.B

S.P.

S.P.s

4.ft.Tk.H.

M.P.

39. Bad weather ruined this southward view from about 1947, but at least we gain a glimpse of the goods yard, which was in use until 7th October 1963. The entrance building is on the right and the house for the station master is on the left. (Stations UK)

40. Only the residence was standing when this record was made on 8th October 1961, during an early stage of electrification. Wrine Hill signal box had been south of here until 25th October 1959. (B.W.L.Brooksbank)

41. Smoke arises from the signal box chimney on a dreary day, 10th January 1990. A class 87 speeds north, with the ex-LNWR workers cottages on the left. The box had 23 levers and was in use from 1875 until 28th June 2004, when the Stoke-on-Trent Signalling Control Centre took over the route from Norton Bridge to here. (A.C.Hartless)

CREWE
Basford Hall Junction

42.   Basford Hall Junction is the first indication that you are approaching Crewe. Here we look south at the gantries in the 1930s. Basford station had been in the far distance until 1st July 1875 and was closed to facilitate quadrupling. The two left posts have fixed distants. (R.S.Carpenter coll.)

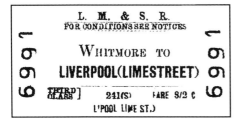

43.   Running south near Basford Hall Junction signal box in August 1944 is "Jubilee" class 4-6-0 no. 5687 *Neptune*. The box opened in 1897 with 80 levers, but these were reduced to 48 later. The frame was still in use in 2012. Basford Sand Siding box had been further south until 12th December 1948. (Bentley coll.)

44.   A DMU provided the service between Stafford and Crewe for many days during the remodelling of the latter in 1985. A unit is approaching the massive array of sidings at Basford Hall. (H.Ballantyne)

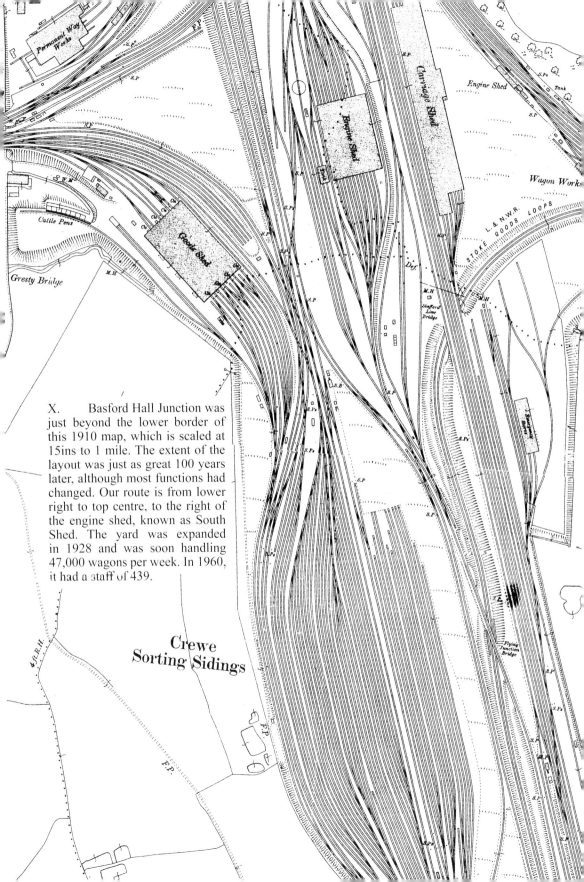

Permanent Way Works

Cattle Pens

Gresty Bridge

Goods Shed

Engine Shed

Carriage Shed

Engine Shed

Tank

Wagon Works

L. & N.W.R. GOODS LOOPS

STOKE

Def.

Stafford Line Bridge

Basford Down

X.　　Basford Hall Junction was just beyond the lower border of this 1910 map, which is scaled at 15ins to 1 mile. The extent of the layout was just as great 100 years later, although most functions had changed. Our route is from lower right to top centre, to the right of the engine shed, known as South Shed. The yard was expanded in 1928 and was soon handling 47,000 wagons per week. In 1960, it had a staff of 439.

Crewe
Sorting Sidings

Flying Junction Bridge

Crewe
South Shed

45.　South Shed had 12 through roads and opened on 1st October 1897. Present on 16th September 1929 were class 1F nos 7272, 7449 and 7435. The "Special Tanks" were built in 1870-80. (H.C.Casserley)

46.　Pictured on 31st May 1947 is 0-8-0 4F class C no. 8962 of LNWR origin. At the northwest corner of the shed was a 50ft turntable. A new roof was provided in 1959. (H.C.Casserley)

47.　Coded 5B, the massive shed was photographed from the south on 10th April 1966, by which time the number of through roads had been reduced to eight. Closure came on 6th November 1967 and the coaling plant in the background soon vanished. (R.S.Carpenter coll.)

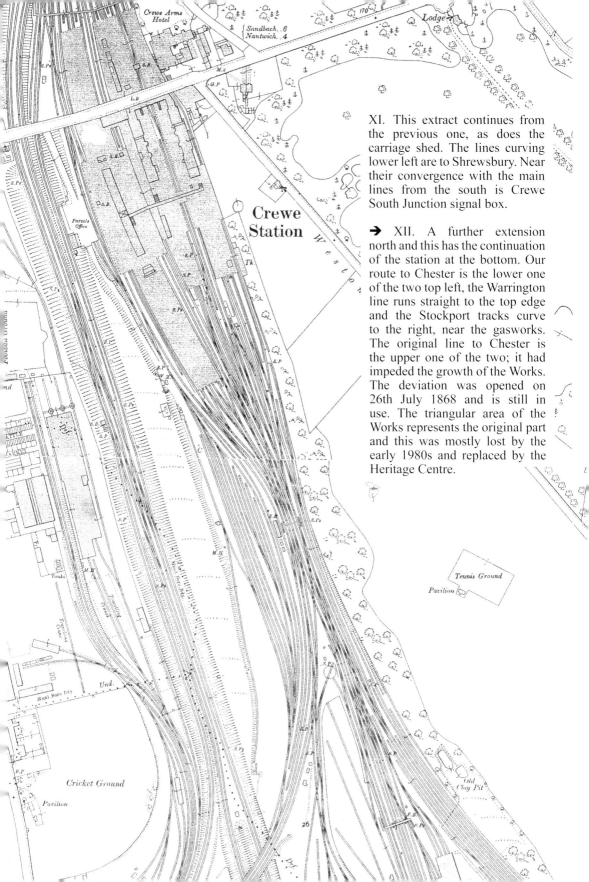

XI. This extract continues from the previous one, as does the carriage shed. The lines curving lower left are to Shrewsbury. Near their convergence with the main lines from the south is Crewe South Junction signal box.

➜ XII. A further extension north and this has the continuation of the station at the bottom. Our route to Chester is the lower one of the two top left, the Warrington line runs straight to the top edge and the Stockport tracks curve to the right, near the gasworks. The original line to Chester is the upper one of the two; it had impeded the growth of the Works. The deviation was opened on 26th July 1868 and is still in use. The triangular area of the Works represents the original part and this was mostly lost by the early 1980s and replaced by the Heritage Centre.

Crewe
Station

Crewe Arms
Hotel

Sandbach..6
Nantwich..4

Lodge

Parcels
Office

Tennis Ground

Pavilion

Cricket Ground

Pavilion

Old
Clay Pit

Crewe Station

48.   The first station had only two tracks, but there were four by the mid-1840s. Rapidly increasing traffic necessitated a major expansion, which began in 1867. Further extensive developments took place around 1887.
(R.M.Casserley coll.)

49.　Modernisation and provision of more through lines took place in 1903-06. These were known as the "Independent Lines" and a third island platform came into being. The glazing eventually covered eight acres and two footbridges.
(Lens of Sutton coll.)

50.　A northward panorama from about 1894 features a train arriving from Chester and also the suspension footbridge provided for access to Crewe Works. It also carried the Works Tramway. The bridge shows on map XII and in photograph no. 53. It lasted until 1939. (R.M.Casserley coll.)

51.   Seen from the north end of one of the platforms is "Claughton" class 4-6-0 no. 110 *Lady Godiva*, coupled to a "Prince of Wales" class and an "Alfred the Great" class. North Shed is behind them, sometime in the 1920s. (R.S.Carpenter coll.)

52.   We are now looking north at the south end of the station, with its outline in the smoke of the 1930s. South Junction Box was completed in 1907 and had a 247 miniature lever power frame. Its replacement had 227 and was in use from 29th September 1940. (R.S.Carpenter coll.)

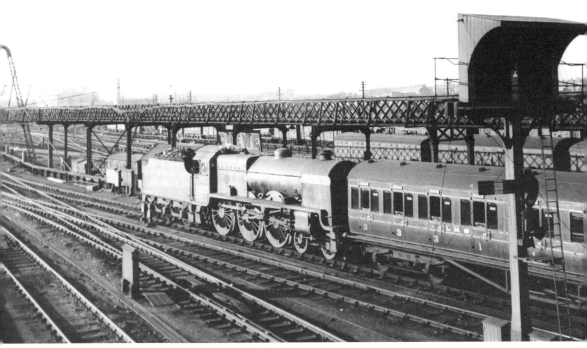

53.	Back to the north end in 1939 and we see "Patriot" class 4-6-0 no. 5529 *Stephenson* with compartment stock and an amazing shadow on the adjacent train. (Bentley coll.)

54.	It is 31st May 1947 and "Princess Coronation" class 4-6-2 no. 6246 *City of Manchester* is about to depart. On the left is North Shed and North Junction Box is in the distance. It had 214 miniature levers and functioned from 25th August 1940 until 21st July 1985. Its predecessor had 266 levers and opened in 1906, replacing an 1878 box with 155 large levers. (H.C.Casserley)

55. Serious railway students admire their subjects under a damaged roof, sometime in 1955. No. 46210 *Lady Patricia* was a 4-6-0 of the "Princess" class. No. 46242 *City of Glasgow* was a 4-6-0 of the "Coronation" class. (Bentley coll.)

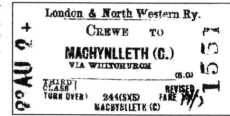

London & North Western Ry.

CREWE   TO

MACHYNLLETH (C.)

VIA WHITCHURCH

(S.O)

THIRD
CLASS
TURN OVER)   244(SXS)

REVISED
FARE

MACHYNLLETH (C)

56.   This is "A" Box on 10th April 1957. Built in 1906, it had a 26-lever miniature frame, which was in use until 21st July 1985. It was later moved to the nearby Heritage Centre and restored to working order. (H.C.Casserley)

57.   "Royal Scot" class 4-6-0 no. 46152 *The King's Dragoon Guardsman* waits to depart with a train from Holyhead on 28th August 1963. (S.Rickard/J&J coll.)

58.   Class 40 no. D307 waits in the bay platform before taking over a Euston to Bangor train on 7th April 1973. Mail traffic was still prolific, evidently. (T.Heavyside)

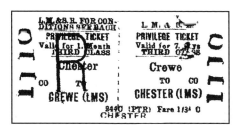

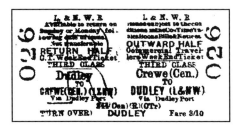

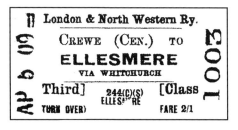

59.   Pictured on 3rd July 1976 is no. 37230 with the 19.14 departure for Cardiff. The irregular features of the roof indicate the complexity of the previous improvements. (T.Heavyside)

60.   It is 5th April 1986 and no. 33020 gets the 14.17 Bangor to Cardiff away from platform 11. Class 33s, once rare away from their native Southern Region, were regular visitors to Crewe in the mid-1980s on Cardiff services. To the left of the train is platform 12, with the disused up bays and disused through down platform comprising the western island beyond. (A.C.Hartless)

61. Based on the Severn Valley Railway, former Southern Region "West Country" class no. 34027 *Taw Valley* makes its debut on the main line to Holyhead on 20th June 1989, with a party of journalists. (H.Ballantyne)

62. No. 87012 *The Royal Bank of Scotland* runs through with a down train on 28th June 1990 and we gain a glimpse of the Victorian architecture of the Crewe Arms Hotel. The LNWR ran it from 1864 onwards. (T.Heavyside)

63.   It is 1st October 1994 and we are looking across four tracks from platform 5 while no. 158858 waits at platform 9, the Chester bay, with the 13.24 to Bangor. Platforms 10, 11 and 12 are beyond, and Rail House is in the background. (A.C.Hartless)

64.   No. 37408 throbs gently as it waits with the 10.48 Holyhead to Birmingham New Street on 13th April 1999. (P.G.Barnes)

65.   The 09.10 Edinburgh to Southampton was hauled by no. 86226 on 22nd February 2001. Virgin stripes are to be seen as it stands at platform 5. The 80mph up and down fast lines (centre) created in the July 2005 remodelling replaced the previous 20/30mph through lines. (D.H.Mitchell)

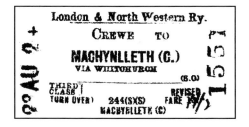

London & North Western Ry.

CREWE   TO

MACHYNLLETH (C.)

VIA WHITCHURCH

(5.0)

THIRD|
CLASS| REVISED
TURN OVER)   244(SXS)   FARE
MACHYNLLETH (C.)

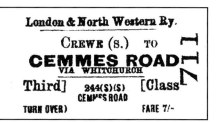

London & North Western Ry.

CREWE (S.)   TO

CEMMES ROAD

VIA WHITCHURCH

Third]   244(S)(S)   [Class
CEMMES ROAD

TURN OVER)   FARE 7/-

66.   Recorded leaving the bay on 7th September 2009 is no. 158826, which is departing for Chester at 12.21. The white building in the distance had served as North Junction Box and had become a key feature of the Heritage Centre. It had 214 levers, whereas its 1906 predecessor had 266. This had the distinction of "Spider Bridge" and its tramway passing through the middle of it; see map XII. (V.Mitchell)

West of the Station

67.   The "Western Memorial" special train was headed by no. 1023 *Western Fusilier* on 29th January 1977 and has just left the station, bound for Chester. It started from Paddington and returned there, with many ears out of the windows much of the time. (T.Heavyside)

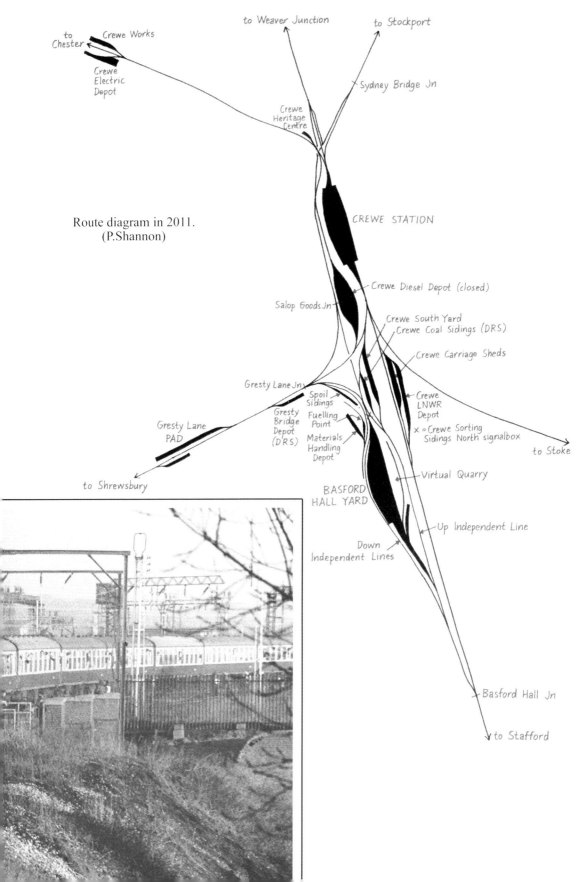

to Chester
Crewe Works
to Weaver Junction
to Stockport
Crewe Electric Depot
Sydney Bridge Jn
Crewe Heritage Centre

Route diagram in 2011.
(P.Shannon)

CREWE STATION

Crewe Diesel Depot (closed)
Salop Goods Jn
Crewe South Yard
Crewe Coal Sidings (DRS)
Crewe Carriage Sheds
Gresty Lane Jn
Spoil Sidings
Fuelling Point
Gresty Bridge Depot (DRS)
Crewe LNWR Depot
Gresty Lane PAD
Materials Handling Depot
x = Crewe Sorting Sidings North signalbox
to Stoke
to Shrewsbury
Virtual Quarry
BASFORD HALL YARD
Up Independent Line
Down Independent Lines
Basford Hall Jn
to Stafford

Crewe North Shed

68.   The fourth shed on the site was completed in 1868, along with a 45ft turntable; it had 14 roads. This was the arrangement in 1938; a steel framed coaling plant was built in 1911 and a concrete one was completed in 1951. (D.K.Jones coll.)

69.   A 70ft turntable was installed in 1948 to replace a 60ft one and to eliminate the turning of the largest engines on triangles. It was situated in a semi-roundhouse, with 32 roads radiating from it, the shed being completed in 1950. This is the scene on 29th May 1960. (R.S.Carpenter)

70.   Brush and English Electric diesels dominated the scene on 15th August 1965, formal shed closure having been on 24th May of that year. There was an allocation of 126 locomotives in 1945; there were 108 steam and 17 diesel-electrics in 1960. (F.Hornby)

Crewe Diesel Depot

71. Five through roads and five short roads were provided in the new shed, which was completed in 1958. It is seen on 29th May 1960. It had 168 diesels in 1976.
(R.S.Carpenter coll.)

Crewe Electric Depot

72. The new facilities were recorded on 22nd September 1965 and a wheel lathe was added in 1994. An open day on 15th October of that year attracted around 12,000 visitors!
(R.S.Carpenter coll.)

Crewe Heritage Centre

73.   On show (from right) on 2nd August 1987 were nos D1041, D5054, 48151, 71000, 6201 and *Bellerophon*. On the left is *Lion*. The Centre was established on the eastern end of the original Works site and was opened by H.M.The Queen on 24th July 1987. (H.Ballantyne)

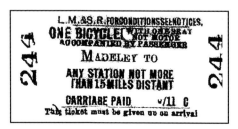

74.   Seen on the same day is the east end of the Centre. From left to right are Hunslet Austerity no. 3694, *Bellerophon* built by Haydock in 1874 and *Lion*. This was created by Todd, Kitson & Laird in 1838. The wiring on the right runs over the Chester route for 1½ miles to serve the Electric Depot. (T.Heavyside)

75.   The Advanced Passenger Train is preserved on the eastern border of the site and is seen on 8th April 1999. A limited selection of coaches was made for the train, which never went into production. (P.G.Barnes)

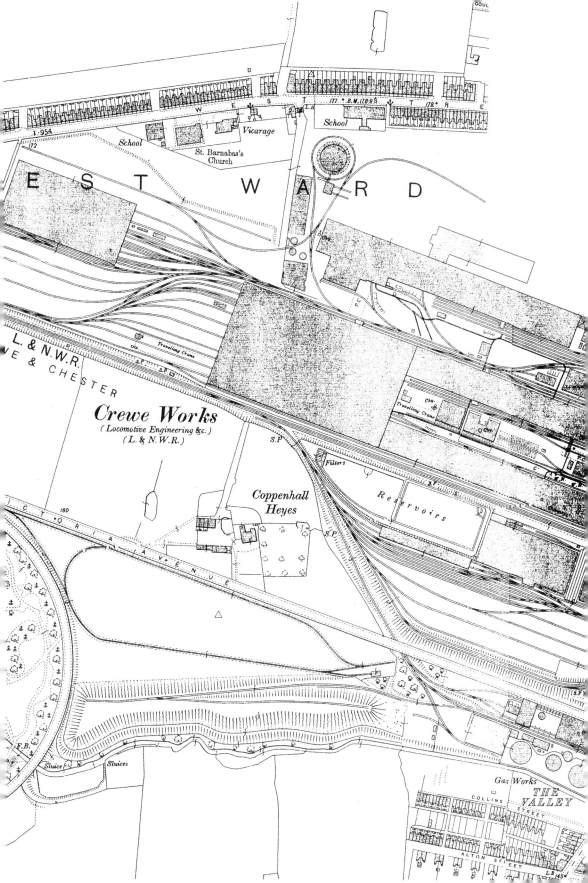

Crewe Works

XIII.　A further continuation of the 1910 map is at a slightly different angle and has the running lines to Chester as the lower pair on the right. Many of the buildings north of it remain in use by the Works. The Electric Maintenance Depot occupies the site south of it. Crewe Steel Works box was built near the word *Works* in 1935 and its 20-lever frame was still in use in 2012. The railway works supplied gas to the entire town until 1952. We have seen one works on the right of map XII; the other is near to the lower border of this one. A third produced gas for kitchen cars and also made lubricating grease.

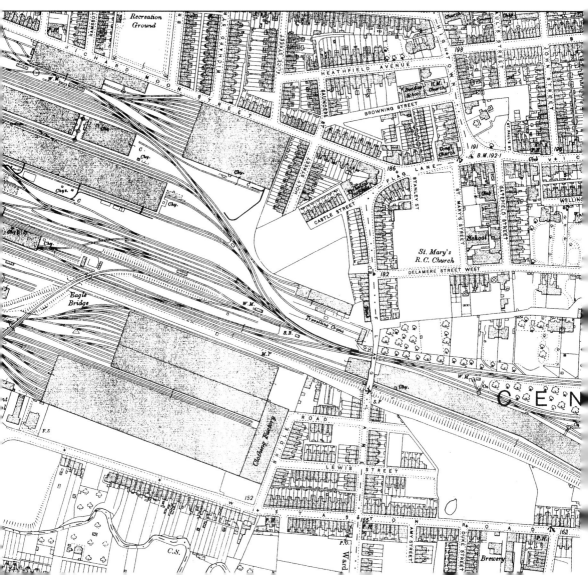

76.   This glimpse inside the Works is from 7th June 1931. The locomotives are class 1P no. 6667 and no. 8783, a class 4F 4-6-0. The Works produced its own steel from about 1890 to 1920, using the Bessemer process. The furnaces had six massive chimneys. (H.C.Casserley)

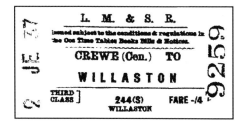

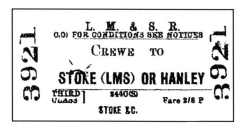

77. The 18ins gauge tramway within the works was extended to the station and ran across the long footbridge of 1878 until 1932. *Midge* was completed in the Works in November 1870. (J.K.Williams coll.)

78. The overhead travelling crane is visible in this view from 7th May 1949. The Beyer-Garratt 2-6-6-2T is no. 7970 and was one of 33 built in 1927-30. The 4000th engine was completed in 1900 and the 7000th in 1950. (H.C.Casserley)

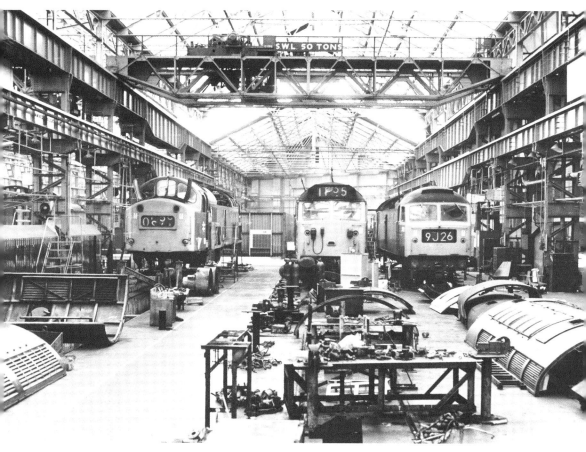

79. A visit to the Erecting Shop was possible during an open day on 18th September 1971. The crane is seen in its entirety, with the driving position left of centre. (T.Heavyside)

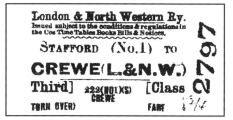

80.   Another open day was held on 17th August 1996 and a record was made of the traverser, which linked the buildings at the west end of the site. (T.Heavyside)

From hereon, readers can enjoy a cab ride in a class 37 on a DVD called *Down the Coast,* available from Middleton Press.

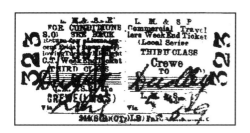

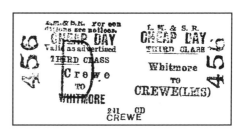

WORLESTON

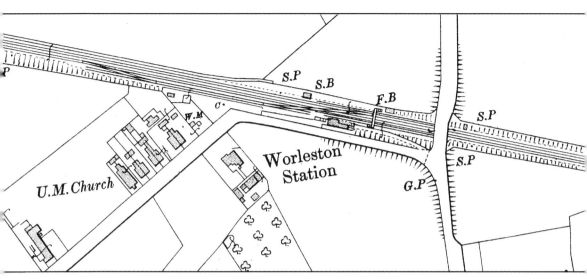

XIV.   The map is from 1910. The station opened as NANTWICH, but after the town received its own station, the name was changed on 1st September 1858 to Worlaston. It was Worleston from about 1862.

81.   Looking towards Crewe, we see the crossover which gave access to the goods yard and meant that shunting movements were undertaken without having facing points on the main line. (P.Laming coll.)

82. The single goods siding is obscured by the locomotive in this postcard shot. Evident is the signal box, which had 15 levers and closed on 4th February 1969. (Lens of Sutton coll.)

83. A westward view in 1950 shows little of the goods yard, which closed on 30th November 1959. Passenger service ceased on 1st September 1952 and no trace remains. (Stations UK)

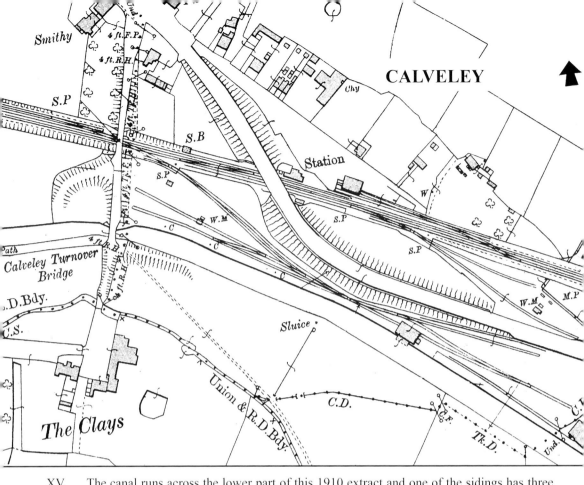

XV.   The canal runs across the lower part of this 1910 extract and one of the sidings has three cranes beside it for transfer traffic. A goods shed serves both.

84.   The bridge over the platforms was built to avoid a level crossing over the goods yard area. The nearby village had a population of 312 in 1901 (Stations UK)

85.   The station opened as Highwayside on 1st October 1840 and was renamed in 1845. Passenger service was withdrawn on 7th March 1960 and this DMU was recorded on 7th June 1965, passing through. (Bentley coll.)

86.   The canal and its gated siding are on the right in this view from the same day. The goods yard beyond the bridge closed on 2nd November 1964. The crane there was rated at 30cwt in 1938, while the one near the canal was listed at 10 tons. (Bentley coll.)

87.   No. 47333 speeds through on 16th August 1975 with the 16.00 Euston to Holyhead. The 30-lever signal box closed on 15th August 1982. There had been another box nearer to Crewe, called Wardle, until 19th August 1966. Little evidence remains here. In the background is a depot of United Dairies, which had a private siding for many years. (T.Heavyside)

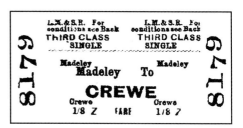

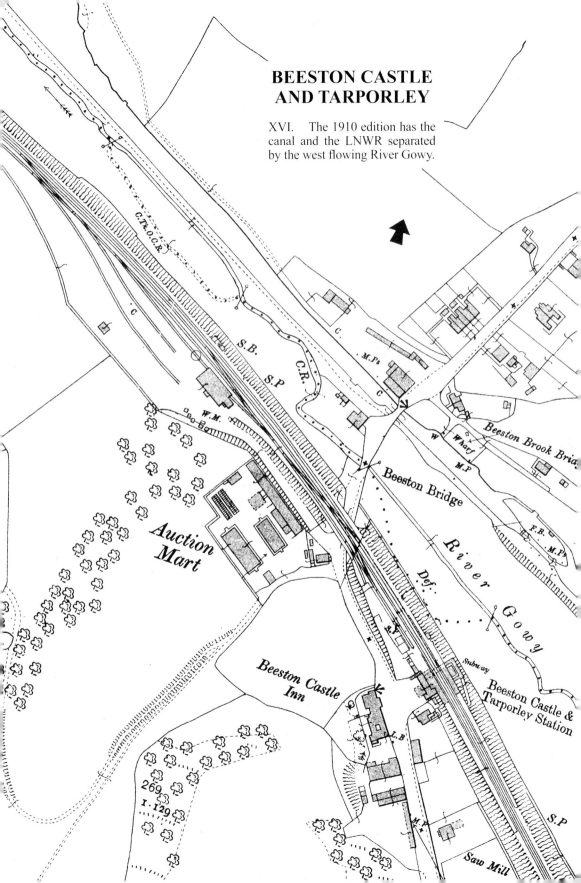

BEESTON CASTLE AND TARPORLEY

XVI.   The 1910 edition has the canal and the LNWR separated by the west flowing River Gowy.

Auction Mart

Beeston Bridge

River Gowy

Beeston Brook Bria

Beeston Castle Inn

Beeston Castle & Tarporley Station

269
I.129

Saw Mill

88.   The lamp was probably a convenient place to tether the "orse", as was so clearly inscribed on the reverse of this postcard. (P.Laming coll.)

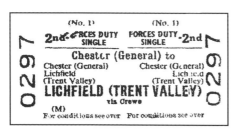

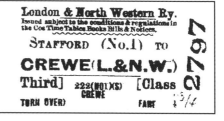

89.   It was an unusual postcard to show four motor vehicles and a comprehensive study of the sanitary provisions. A subway was provided to the up platform. (P.Laming coll.)

90.   The first named village had 259 residents in 1961. Both of the extensive canopies have unusual glazed panels at both ends. (R.M.Casserley)

91.　　Modernisation was recorded on 22nd August 1964 in the form of flat bottom rails and electric lighting. No buildings now remain. (R.M.Casserley)

92.　　Passenger service ceased on 18th April 1966 and goods facilities were withdrawn on 4th January 1965. The yard was photographed in 1968. (Stations UK)

93.　　No. 47533 is passing by with the 13.20 Holyhead to Euston on 16th August 1975. The 1915 signal box had a 26-lever frame and was still in use in 2012. (T.Heavyside)

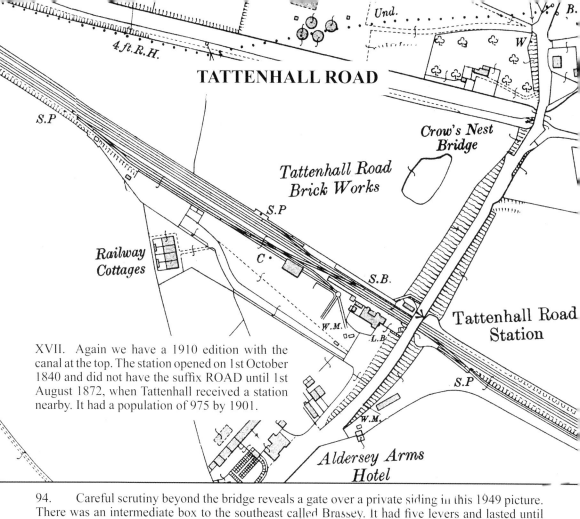

TATTENHALL ROAD

4ft.R.H.

S.P

Tattenhall Road
Brick Works

Crow's Nest
Bridge

Und.

W

S.P

C

Railway
Cottages

S.B.

W.M.

L.B.

Tattenhall Road
Station

S.P

XVII. Again we have a 1910 edition with the
canal at the top. The station opened on 1st October
1840 and did not have the suffix ROAD until 1st
August 1872, when Tattenhall received a station
nearby. It had a population of 975 by 1901.

W.M.

Aldersey Arms
Hotel

94. Careful scrutiny beyond the bridge reveals a gate over a private siding in this 1949 picture.
There was an intermediate box to the southeast called Brassey. It had five levers and lasted until
29th April 1966. (Stations UK)

95.   One more 1949 view and this includes the long up refuge siding, plus much of the goods yard, which closed on 4th January 1965. The signal box was replaced by a new one in 1951. (Stations UK)

96.   This 1957 photograph features the 30-lever 1951 box, which lasted until 27th August 1967. Passenger service was withdrawn on 15th September 1966. Further north were boxes at Malpas and Broxton, both closing on 16th December 1963. Then came Tattenhall Junction, which lasted until 27th February 1983. It had 30 levers. (Stations UK)

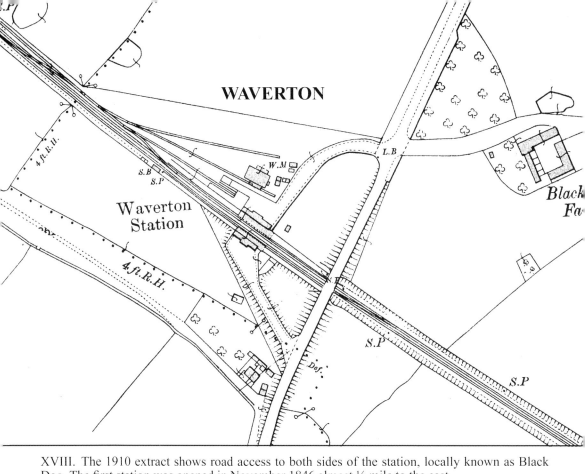

XVIII. The 1910 extract shows road access to both sides of the station, locally known as Black Dog. The first station was opened in November 1846 almost ½ mile to the east.

97.   Symmetrical proportions, fine finials, palatial chimneys and stylish toilet ventilators combine to give a great visual pleasure. Sadly almost all was lost. (P.Laming coll.)

98. A panorama from 1949 includes much of the goods yard, which was closed on 1st March 1965. The station was paid for by the Duke of Westminster and was opened in 1887. (Stations UK)

99. More of the details can be enjoyed in this 1957 record, including small dummy dormers. Passenger traffic ceased on 15th June 1959. The signal box had a 30-lever frame and was in use until 23rd May 1971. (Stations UK)

100.   Christleton Tunnel is 160yds in length and "Royal Scot" class 4-6-0 no. 6117 *Welsh Guardsman* is emerging from it in about 1931, with a down express. (R.S.Carpenter coll.)

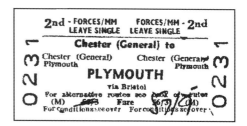

101.　We are looking north at about the same time. The ex-LNWR Christleton box had 10 levers and was used until 29th April 1966. The Shropshire Union Canal passes over the tunnel - see map XIX lower right. (R.S.Carpenter coll.)

Extract from *Bradshaw's Guide 1866* (reprinted by Middleton Press)

CHESTER.

A telegraph station.

HOTEL.—Albion.

MARKET DAYS.—Wednesday and Saturday.

FAIRS.—Last Thursday in February, July 5th, and October 10th.　RACES in May and October.

CHESTER is a genuine Roman city, built four-square, within walls, which remain to this day. It is also a cathedral town and borough, with 31,110 population, returning two members, a peer, the Prince of Wales, who bears the title of Earl of Chester, and the capital of Cheshire, on the river Dee, thirteen miles from Liverpool, where four lines meet. The joint station, which cost nearly a quarter of a million, is 1,010 feet long. Chester, so called by the Saxons because of the camp, or *castram* here, was named *Deva* by the Romans, who joined it by a road right across the country to Colchester, called the *Via Deva*. Two main streets were cut by them into the rock, terminating in the four city gates; above these on both sides are lines of shops and covered ways, called the *Rows*, to which you ascend by a few steps. Several old timber buildings with gable fronts are seen. *St. John's* is the oldest of its eleven or twelve churches, having solid Norman pillars, &c. The *Cathedral*, built of the red sandstone so common here; the west front, not older than the 16th century, is the best part of it. A beautiful early English *Chapter House* is close by. The bishop's throne was the shrine of St. Werburgh, founder of the abbey here.

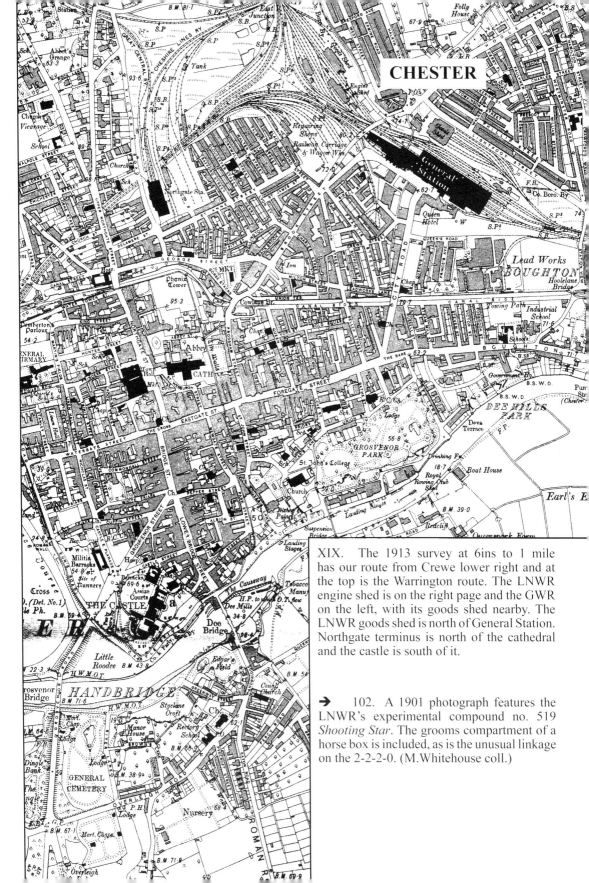

CHESTER

XIX. The 1913 survey at 6ins to 1 mile has our route from Crewe lower right and at the top is the Warrington route. The LNWR engine shed is on the right page and the GWR on the left, with its goods shed nearby. The LNWR goods shed is north of General Station. Northgate terminus is north of the cathedral and the castle is south of it.

→   102. A 1901 photograph features the LNWR's experimental compound no. 519 *Shooting Star*. The grooms compartment of a horse box is included, as is the unusual linkage on the 2-2-2-0. (M.Whitehouse coll.)

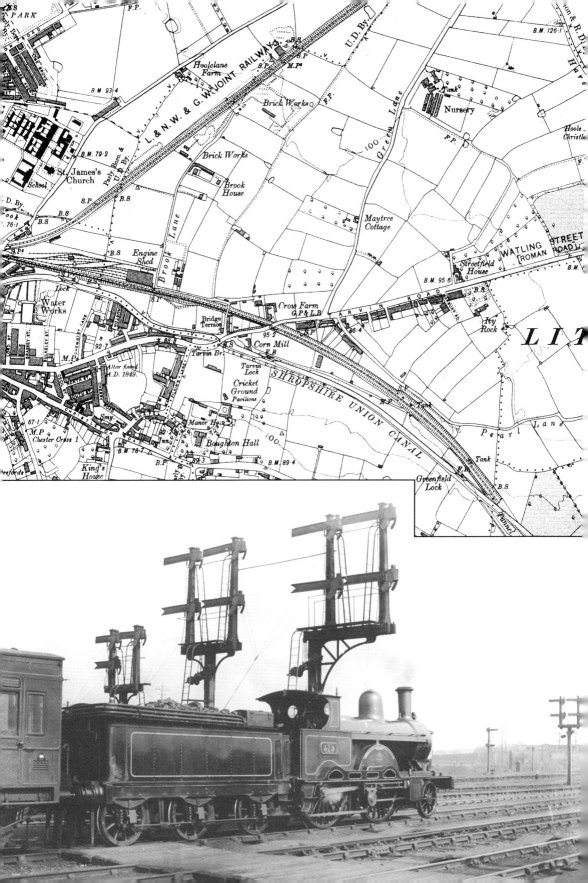

103.   Passing the LNWR water tank in about 1932 is 4-6-0 no. 5652 *Oryx*, bound for Crewe. The engine shed is beyond the right border. (R.M.Casserley coll.)

104. In this undated view are nos 1447 *Gillah*, 675, 622 and 2279. The eight-road shed was opened by the LNWR in 1870, with a 42ft turntable nearby. (R.M.Casserley coll.)

105. This picture is dated June 1935, but the stock is not numbered. The shed was reroofed in 1944 and closed on 5th June 1967. (R.M.Casserley coll.)

106.   A photograph from around 1951 confirms the pre-nationalisation ownership. Dating from the opening, the building was still in good order in the 21st century. (Milepost 92½)

107.   This eastward panorama is from 1st August 1959 and includes No. 2 Box. It had 182 levers and was in use from 1890. (Bentley coll.)

108.   No. 2 Box is seen more clearly on 26th November 1964, but the station is unclear, due to steam and smoke. Box closure came on 6th May 1984. (R.J.Essery/R.S.Carpenter)

109.   Minutes later, class 8F 2-8-0 no. 48255 accelerates a train of empty mineral wagons, bound for Crewe. (R.J.Essery/R.S.Carpenter)

110.　A train from North Wales departs behind class 40 no. 245 on 7th July 1973, bound for Crewe. On the right is No. 1 Box, which served from 23rd February 1958 until 16th September 1973. It had 60 levers. The Warrington lines are in front of it. (T.Heavyside)

→　111. The massive goods shed was on the north side of the station and was photographed on 4th June 1974. It had been built by the LNWR. Coal and general goods traffic ceased here on 30th November 1970. (R.S.Carpenter)

→　112. Nos 44008 and 24133 appeared on 21st January 1978 with the "Peak Commemorative Tour" from Nottingham. The Warrington lines are on the left. (T.Heavyside)

Other views can be found in the *Chester to Rhyl, Shrewsbury to Chester, Chester to Birkenhead* and *Chester Tramways* albums.

113.   No. 47423 is bound for Holyhead on 14th July 1979 and we gain a view of No. 3A Box and the roof of the former LNWR goods shed. Near its point rodding is a hose for filling train toilets. (H.C.Casserley)

114.   On 8th August 1983, we witness no. 47331 running through with a Freightliner from Holyhead. Behind it is No. 2 Box. On the right is part of the Chester Power Signal Box which opened on 4th May 1984. (D.H.Mitchell)

115.   Arriving on 13th June 1988 is no. 150118 forming the 17.28 Crewe to Holyhead service. It is entering platform 3; no. 1 is on the right. The Power Signal Box is on the left border. (T.Heavyside)

116.   The 14.39 Holyhead to Birmingham New Street was formed of more substantial stock on 12th April 1999. No. 37421 was on hire from EWS. On the right are the bays numbered 5 and 6, which could take five coaches each. (P.G.Barnes)

117. Platform 4 is featured again and the 13.17 Bangor to Crewe is seen on 23rd July 2001, worked by no. 150145. Beyond the right border is platform 7A/7B, the track of which had received a conductor rail in 1993 for Wirral trains. (A.C.Hartless)

118. The 14.17 Crewe to Holyhead is seen from platform 4 on the same day. The 1848 building is behind the train and buddleias abound. The class 175 units were introduced in 2000 and were unreliable initially. They were replaced temporarily, as seen in picture 116. (A.C.Hartless)

119.   This is the rear of the 13.35 Holyhead to Crewe on 3rd October 2006. The DMU is no. 158660 and it is at platform 4, amidst the amazing architecture. (A.C.Hartless)

120.   More of the 1848 structure is evident on 26th June 2012, but the adjacent platform is unnumbered, as it was latterly not used by passengers. No. 150241 is about to work to Crewe from this unique and historical location. (H.Ballantyne)

MP Middleton Press

EVOLVING THE ULTIMATE RAIL ENCYCLOPEDIA

Easebourne Lane, Midhurst, West Sussex.
GU29 9AZ   Tel:01730 813169

www.middletonpress.co.uk   email:info@middletonpress.co.uk
A-978 0 906520 B- 978 1 873793 C- 978 1 901706 D-978 1 904474
E - 978 1 906008   F- 978 1 908174

All titles listed below were in print at time of publication - please check current availability by looking at our
website - *www.middletonpress.co.uk* or by requesting a Brochure which includes our
LATEST RAILWAY TITLES also our TRAMWAY, TROLLEYBUS, MILITARY and COASTAL series